*If I could be given any gift imaginable, one that would make me happy beyond words... the gift I'd choose would be you, Daughter... each and every time.*

— Terry Bairnson

Dear Rachel,
Happy Valentine's
Day with love,
lots of Mom

25¢

— for my special —
daughter in my
always
heart.
I love you.

# A Daughter
## *Is Life's*
## *Greatest Gift*

Words to Let a
Daughter Know She Is
in Your Heart Forever

Edited by Patricia Wayant

**Blue Mountain Press**™
Boulder, Colorado

We wish to thank Susan Polis Schutz for permission to reprint the following poems that appear in this publication: "You Make Every One of My Days Brighter," "You Will Always Be My Beautiful Daughter," and "Daughter, I Am So Proud of You." Copyright © 1986, 1998 by Stephen Schutz and Susan Polis Schutz. All rights reserved.

Library of Congress Control Number: 2007908210
ISBN: 978-1-59842-258-0

▌ and Blue Mountain Press are registered in U.S. Patent and Trademark Office.
Certain trademarks are used under license.

Acknowledgments appear on page 92.

Printed in China.
Second Printing: 2009

✪ This book is printed on recycled paper.

This book is printed on archival quality, white felt, 110 lb. paper. This paper has been specially produced to be acid free (neutral pH) and contains no groundwood or unbleached pulp. It conforms with the requirements of the American National Standards Institute, Inc., so as to ensure that this book will last and be enjoyed by future generations.

# Blue Mountain Arts, Inc.
P.O. Box 4549, Boulder, Colorado 80306

# Contents

# A Daughter
# Is Life's Greatest Gift

A daughter is one of the greatest gifts
    one could ever have
She begins her life loving and trusting you
    automatically

For many years, you are the center of her life
Together you experience the delights of
    the new things she learns and does

You enter into her play and are once again young
And even though it's harder to enter into her
    world as she becomes a teen...

You are there, understanding her dilemmas and
    her fears
And wishing with all your heart that she didn't
    have to go through them...

A daughter's smile is a precious sight that
    you treasure each time you see it
And the sound of her laughter always brings
    joy to your heart

Her successes mean more to you than your own
And her happiness is your happiness

Her heartaches and disappointments
    become yours, too
Because when she isn't okay, you can't
    be okay either

Daughters aren't perfect
  but you, Daughter, come close to it
You have given me more happiness than you know

I am thankful for your kindness and
    thoughtfulness
And I am proud of who you are
    and how you live your life

Words can't express how much you mean
    to me or how much I love you
The love goes too deep, and the gratitude
    and pride I feel are boundless

You are my life's greatest gift

— Barbara Cage

# My Daughter,
## There Is So Much
### to Love
### About You

You are beautiful, intelligent,
generous, helpful, and kind —
a shining star in my eyes.
Your sparkling personality
    lights up a room,
and when you are near,
    spirits are lifted.
It is said that we all need a little joy
every day of our lives.
Well, with the gift of you,
I have a lot of joy every single minute.
With you, I have a beautiful,
    special daughter
who brings so many blessings
    to my heart.

— Jacqueline Schiff

# I Wish You Could See Yourself Through My Eyes

In you, I see a gorgeous butterfly
    emerging from her cocoon,
Someone who is growing
    and changing.
I see a young woman who is ready
To take on the world and
Whatever it throws her way.
I see someone who stands up for herself
And for those she loves,
Someone who offers
A helpful hand,
A shoulder to cry on,
And a kind word when she knows
    someone is down.
I see an angel here on earth.

— Shannon Koehler

When I look at you, Daughter,
I see someone who has the courage
and strength to overcome many
obstacles. No matter how many times
you fall, you get up again. Even when
you want to give up, you don't.

I see someone who has a big heart.
You make everyone around you feel
loved. You touch so many lives
without even knowing it.

I see someone who has been blessed
with not only outer beauty but inner
beauty. This is the kind of beauty that
is everlasting. Time can never take
that away from you.

— Mary Adisano

# *You Make Every One of My Days Brighter*

My day becomes wonderful
when I see your
pretty face smiling so sweetly
There is such warmth and intelligence
radiating from you
It seems that every day
you grow smarter and more beautiful
and every day
I am more proud of you

As you go through different stages of life
you should be aware that there will be
    many times
when you will feel scared and confused
but with your strength and values
you will always end up wiser
and you will have grown from
    your experiences
understanding more about people and life
I have already gone through
these stages
So if you need advice or someone to talk to
to make sense out of it all
I hope that you will talk to me
as I am continually cheering
    for your happiness
my sweet daughter

— Susan Polis Schutz

# What Being Your Parent Means to Me

It means that I have had the opportunity to experience loving someone more than I love myself. I have learned what it's like to experience pleasure and pain through someone else's life.

It has brought me pride and joy; your accomplishments touch me and thrill me like no one else's can. It has brought me a few tears and heartaches at times, but it has taught me hope and patience. It has shown me the depth, strength, and power of love.

It hasn't always been easy, and I'm sure I've said and done things that have hurt or confused you. But no one has ever made me as satisfied as you do just by being happy. No one has made me as proud as you do just by living up to your responsibilities.

No one's smile has ever warmed my heart like yours does; no one's laughter fills me with delight as quickly as yours can. No one's hugs feel as sweet, and no one's dreams mean as much to me as yours do.

No other memories of bad times have miraculously turned into important lessons or humorous stories; the good times have become precious treasures to relive again and again.

You are a part of me, and no matter what happened in the past or what the future holds, you are someone I will always accept, forgive, appreciate, adore, and love unconditionally.

Being your parent means that I've been given one of life's greatest gifts: you.

— Barbara Cage

# Even Before You
# Were Born,
# I Dreamed of Having
# a Daughter like You

One dreams of having a daughter
for many reasons —
some simple,
some sweet,
some silly.
I wanted you so I could share what's good
    about our world:
fat puppies and perfect peaches,
music and magnolias,
hummingbirds and harvest moons and hugs.
I wanted you so I could share what's good
    about growing up:
families sharing autumn picnics,
romping in the snow,
feeling safe, feeling proud, and feeling loved.
I wanted you so I could share what's good
    about being a girl:
frilly dresses and French braids,
whispering and secrets,
double dates and Nancy Drew and malls.
Here's to dreams coming true, my daughter!
(Yours, as well as mine.)

— Jayne Jaudon Ferrer

# *Every Day I Am Thankful to Have You as My Child*

On the day you were born, my life changed in so many unbelievable ways. In that one special moment when I first felt your breath on my cheek, I realized my life would never be the same. For the rest of my life I was going to have this incredible person to love, nourish, and protect. Even the way you looked at me told me so many things about the happiness I felt. The way your little hand held on to mine assured me that loneliness would never come my way again, and your beautiful smile always let me know you were glad I was there.

Even though it was so long ago, it's still fresh in my mind. I still feel this way today. All the love you brought me then has grown along with you. Every single day, I am thankful to have you as my child. I cannot imagine anything being more rewarding or wonderful than watching you grow and knowing I have done my best to help you get through each and every step you have taken in your life.

Thank you for giving me the opportunity to feel this way. Having you as my child is a treasure that was placed in my heart and in my life on the day you were born.

— Debra Heintz

# What It Means
# to Have a Daughter

Throughout the years, just watching
my daughter grow from childhood
to adulthood has brought me more
pleasure than anyone could ever know.
From her, I have learned that life's most
precious gift is the family around us.

— Linda E. Knight

Having a daughter means placing her comfort
   before your own.
It means trying your best every moment of
   every day to shelter her from harm.
It means worrying endlessly, and
   sometimes needlessly, about her and
   everything that enters her life.
It means wanting only the best for her
   and aching inside at those times when
   things go wrong.
It means giving her all that you have to give
   and feeling her special love fill your
   heart more deeply than you ever imagined.
It means loving her without reserve, and
   with all that you are, for the rest of your life.

— Linda Sackett-Morrison

# A Daughter
# like You...

To have a daughter like you is to
feel gratified when I wake up each
day. You have walked the path to
success and triumphed with your
positive attitude, your talents, and
the lessons you learned.

To have a daughter like you is to feel
peace in my heart. I don't have to
hover over you, worry needlessly
about you, or wonder if you're safe
and secure. In the depths of my soul,
I know you are a strong, capable,
accomplished woman who is exactly
where she wants to be in her life.

To have a daughter like you is to
hear the music of fun and laughter
wherever I go. Your can-do attitude,
boundless energy, and enthusiasm
for making the best of every situation
are contagious and fun. Your spirited
nature uplifts and inspires me.

To have a daughter like you is to
be in the company of a best friend
who holds my hand, gives me hugs,
and walks with me through my
troubles. In you, I have a special
companion who shares with me a
special understanding of why we are
blessed to be friends.

To have a daughter like you is to
walk with happiness in my heart for
all we share.

— Jacqueline Schiff

# *Please Know and Remember...*

**W**henever I think of you,
I find so many hopes and
memories in my heart. Those
thoughts and remembrances...
they're my favorite treasures,
and nothing warms my heart
like they do.

— Terry Bairnson

It is with the greatest joy
that I am your guardian,
protector, and nurturer.
I will always strive to fulfill
these roles with honor, trust,
and respect for your thoughts,
feelings, and individuality.
What matters most in life are the
people you love, and, for always,
you will be one of the people in
my life whom I love the most.
You are the true meaning of life.
You are a dream with all its hope
and promise.
You are love, endless and pure.

— Linda Sackett-Morrison

# If I Could,
# I'd Give You All the Best
# Life Can Offer

If I could, I'd give you everlasting things — like sunny thoughts to lift you high above your troubles and warm rays of love and friendship always in your heart.

If I could shower you with happiness each hour, I would. I would wrap you in protective ways, making sure no problem ever touched your life or displaced your joy for living. I would take your hand and lead you securely down life's path, safely shielding you from any harm.

I'd do all this for you, if only the power were in my hands. But I hope you'll see that life's very best is yours already — beginning with your independent nature and the power to choose your own way to find happiness.

All the same, my best gift to you will be as it has always been: my great love for you and my belief that you will choose your paths in life with honor and integrity, just as you always have.

— Barbara J. Hall

# I Will Always Want What's Best for You

I often find myself deep in thought,
wondering where life will lead you.
Will you make the right choices
    or the wrong ones?
Will the mistakes you make
    cost you more
than you intend on paying?
There are so many concerns,
    and I know my worries are endless.

As your parent I want to protect you,
    but I realize that I cannot.
I know you must make your own decisions,
regardless of what I believe to be right.
Whatever you decide, I will
    support you and be there for you
        with all my love.
I trust in you, just as I know
    you trust in yourself,
and I will respect your choices.
No matter what,
    you have always followed
        your dreams
and held on to what
    you believe in.
You are my heart and soul.
You are my child.

— Judith Trocchia-Cincotta

# I Hope You'll Keep Flying to the Heights of Your Dreams

Once you were a little girl who believed you could be anything — from a princess to a pet doctor. Nothing could stop you from flying fearlessly to where children's dreams come true. You were certain that your wishes would take you to the magical places where you needed to be.

Today, you are a young woman who is not always so sure of her destiny. Your dreams have been tempered by reality and challenged by people who tried to clip your wings. But you always bounce back with all the passion of that little girl inside you — the one who believes she'll make her dreams come true.

I hope you'll always keep on fighting for your right to be "you." Keep being real in the way you live, and keep flying to the heights of your dreams. Pass fearlessly by anyone who tells you, "You can't do that," and find those places where you can always use your unique gifts. Honor that little girl inside you.

— Jacqueline Schiff

# Daughter, I Am
# So Proud of You

You have continually
demonstrated your
incredible intelligence, creativity
and ability to work very hard
Your accomplishments
have soared
You have risen
to heights
way beyond your years
I am so proud of you —
of your noble morals
your strength
and your sensitivity

You are a very special individual
because you are able to
stick so firmly to your principles
I think you have discovered
who you are, however —
I want to be sure that
you are in touch
with your heart and emotions
as well as your intellect
so that you will be
able to develop the kinds
of close relationships that
together with your accomplishments
will make you truly happy
Your soft sensitive side
will need to blend with your
worldly side
And you will need to learn to
ignore the mean words of others
as well as their excessive praises
You, not other people
must be the judge of your life
And in the future
I hope you can spend
more time being free
to do what you want
You are a very creative spirit
who needs to fly more
I am proud of you
and I love you

— Susan Polis Schutz

# This Girl of Mine

My boy came like rain —
expected and needed.
There was no thought to love;
it was just like the beautiful tea-stained
birthmark that leaked onto his tiny stomach,
like his fluid blue eyes that searched
for the next good meaning.
As soon as he could hold a book — he did.
We read to the heart-like ticking of the clock,
the steady, wintry hum of the furnace.
He listened to what I had to say
like I was a sage, a song, a mother.
I knew I'd never love another child,
not like that.

Still, two years later came my girl —
a girl who grabbed for life the way
dawn grabs for light.
When she was able,
I put a book in her tiny hands
and she threw it across the room —
threw it like it was an old toy,
a handful of wilted flowers,
a slightly broken heart.
How could this be?
This girl of mine
who doesn't love to read,
who doesn't love the weighty feel,
the inky, rooty smell,
the brainy, secret nerve of books?
Well... she loves the things outside of books.
She loves the things that books are about.

A teenager now,
she still hugs as loud as she yells.
She has a garden of friends,
girls like her.
They have brittle, dramatic conversations.
She feels so bad, so bad,
for a friend who has been forgotten
by a boyfriend.
But I can tell she doesn't really feel that bad.
I can tell she's just trying on compassion,
like one of those balled-up sweaters
in the corner of her whirlwind room.
I hope she'll choose compassion.
I think she will, her brown eyes are filled
with refracting pools of wild love.

In the city she links my arm tightly with hers
and kisses my cheek, which surprises me —
as if a butterfly has quickly landed there.
When she was little, her legs ached often —
she'd cry and say her legs felt wobbly.
But her legs aren't wobbly anymore;
they're strong and quick.
Her feet click along in high-heeled,
polka-dotted shoes,
going where she wills them to go,
fearless, fast, and headlong into life.

I don't just love her.
I fall in love with her every day.

— Jenny Scott

# For My Daughter
# Who Loves Animals

Once a week, whether the money is there
or not, I write a check for her lessons.
But today, as I waited in the car for her
to finish her chores, after she had wrapped
this one's delicate legs, brushed burrs
and caked mud from that one's tail,
I saw her stop and offer her body
to a horse's itchy head. One arm up,
she gave him the whole length of her side.

And he knew the gesture, understood
the gift, stepped in close on oiled hooves
and pressed his head to her ribcage.
From hip to armpit he raked her body until,
to keep from falling, she leaned into him
full weight, her foot braced
against a tack post for balance.
Before horses, it was snakes, coiled
around her arms like African bracelets.
And before that, stray dogs, cats
of every color, even the misfits,
the abandoned and abused.
It took me so long to learn how to love,
how to give myself up and over to another.
Now I see how she has always
loved them all, snails and spiders,
from the very beginning, without fear or shame,
saw even the least of them, ants,
gnats, heard and answered
even the slightest of their calls.

— Dorianne Laux

# You're More Than My Daughter... You're My Friend

Through the years, I watched you grow, change, and constantly question everything. When you were little, there was an overwhelming feeling inside me that wanted to hold you close and keep you safe and warm all your life. Yet as the years passed, I realized that I couldn't do that.

Now, after years of letting you go your own way and watching you become a beautiful young lady, our roles have changed. You are still my daughter and I am still your parent, but most precious of all is the fact that we have become good friends and we have a friendship that will stand the test of time.

I'll always cherish the wonder and joy of watching you grow into a beautiful young lady. I'll always be proud to say, "This is my daughter." But most of all, I'm proud to say that you are my best friend.

— Vicky Lafleur

# *My Favorite Woman*

After we've spent the day together,
we talk for hours on the phone;
there is always more to say.

She is the only person
I can comfortably shop with
and not feel impatient
when she tries on things forever
or worry that I'm taking too long
in deciding between two dresses.

Only with her can I still giggle,
mostly at the silliest things.
I don't offer to shorten anyone else's hems
nor tidy up anyone else's kitchen.
When she borrows something,
I don't ask for it back.

We exchange recipes,
gossip about family members,
and reminisce about the past.

When she criticizes, it matters.
Her compliments mean more
than those of friends.

She is my favorite woman to be with.
I am talking about my daughter.

— Natasha Josefowitz

# A Little Prayer
## I'd Love to Share
### with You

I want your life to be such a wonderful one.
I wish you peace, deep within your soul;
joyfulness in the promise of each new day;
stars to reach for, dreams to come true, and
memories more beautiful than words can say.

I wish you friends close at heart, even over
    the miles;
loved ones — the best treasures we're
    blessed with;
present moments to live in, one day
    at a time;
serenity, with its wisdom; courage,
    with its strength;
and new beginnings, to give life a chance
    to really shine.

I wish you understanding — of how special
    you really are;
a journey, safe from the storms and warmed
    by the sun;
a path to wonderful things;
an invitation, to the abundance life brings;
and an angel watching over, for all the days
    to come.

— Douglas Pagels

# What a Dad Will Do for His Daughter

What a dad will do for his daughter is
    rock his sick baby girl
until the sun peeks through the darkness
letting him know the night of worry is over.
He will take her small hand in his
    and walk slowly as she takes her first
walk to the ice-cream shop to share
    a cone full of heaven on earth.
He will sip from the tiny tea cup she has set
    in front of him,
and in harmony with the stuffed animals
    carefully placed in their seats,
he will sing the praises of her great hospitality.
He will sit through dance recitals and fashion shows
where he is the only audience
and will clap with the enthusiasm of a
    thousand people.
He will take her fishing and play soccer
and introduce her to the world outside
as if just experiencing it for the first time himself.
Perhaps he is.
He will sit with her through sweat and tears
    over homework
that was supposed to be turned in the day before,
and he'll smile as they finish, seeing her relief.
He will place a firm hand on the shoulder of the
    young man that comes
to take her to the school dance
silently letting him know where he stands and
    what he expects.

He will watch with overflowing pride as his young lady
accepts her high school diploma
and will silently pray to God to calm his fears
and get him through the day.
He will be full of conversation and more
    than happy to listen
when she calls home now and then —
even when the game of the year is on.
He will gently fold her arm around his
and with all the courage and faith
    he can hold on to
he will stroll down the aisle,
giving her hand but keeping her youth.
He will be the first one in the maternity ward,
at the nursery window,
carefully inspecting the activities of
    his new family member —
another part of her, another part of him.
He will reassure her as time rages on
and the signs of his old age start to frighten her.
He will caress her hand with a passion
to which she has never felt
as he whispers his last wishes to her.
He will come to her heart for all her life
as she sees his manner in herself
or his features in her children.
He will live in the smiles
that grace her face
as she remembers the things he did for her.

— Cheryl D'Aprix

# *I'm Going to Be Here for You, No Matter What*

When you need someone to turn to, I'll be here for you. I will do whatever it takes and give as much as I can... to help you find your smile and get you back on steady ground again.

When you just need to talk, I will listen with my heart. And I will do my best to hear the things you may want to say, but can't quite find the words for.

I will never betray the trust you put in me. All I will do is keep on caring and doing my best to see you through. If there are decisions to be made, I may offer a direction to go in. If there are tears to be dried, I will tenderly dry them.

Your happiness and peace of mind are so closely interwoven with mine that they are inseparable. I will truly, deeply, and completely care about you every day. You can count on that.

— Douglas Pagels

# Find Your Special Place, Daughter

Virginia Woolf once said
we all need a room of our own.
Perhaps not a room but,
    most definitely,
        a place —
"where neither moth nor rust doth corrupt,
where thieves do not break through nor steal."
A heaven on earth,
    if you will —
        a revitalizing place to retreat
            when frustration and fatigue
            close in like hungry vultures,
someplace where there isn't any trouble,
someplace where your heart is nourished,
someplace where your soul is fed,
    someplace that feels like Home.

My place is
    my mother's back porch, at dusk —
        mist nuzzling the brown cows
        in the pasture sprawled green and lush
    at the foot of a mountain...
        tree frogs singing rounds with cicadas,
        their vibrating chorus
    an aural yin and yang account of
        events of the day.
And as the last pink streaks of sky ebb to gray,
    the firefly light show commences —
        yellow polka dots flashing lazily
        like coy lanterns
            dancing in the darkening stillness.

Find your retreat, my darling,
    that place of escape and
        assured restoration
    that will set you free,
        make you whole,
            take you home.
We mothers worry about so many things —
    *are you safe? are you satisfied?*
    *are you happy? are you loved?* —
but we worry less if we know
    that wherever life leads,
    whatever it brings,
there's a place you call Home
    in your heart.
                        — Jayne Jaudon Ferrer

# Life Lessons on the Road to Your Dreams

Treasure your dreams; like your life, they are a wonderful gift. Accept and appreciate that you're the one most responsible for making them come true. Be your own best friend. Cheer yourself on.

Choose your thoughts, because if you don't, you're still making a choice and you'll have to take what you get. In your mind's eye, create a positive picture that will draw what you want to you. Your intuition is powerful; use it. Keep your desires burning. Don't be afraid to take careful chances.

Inform yourself. Make the connection between your thoughts, your actions, and the results you're getting. The cumulative quality of your actions will weave the tapestry of your destiny. Live your life consciously; don't just let your life live you.

Look at your circumstances as life lessons rather than adversities. Keep a careful watch over your joy. Cherish it. Acknowledge your blessings, no matter how small they may seem. You are a student in the school of life and in many ways your own teacher. Appreciate the lessons you've learned, and enjoy life, others, and yourself.

— Donna Fargo

# *Keep Reaching for the Stars*

Day by day, year by year
I've watched you grow
I've watched you grabbing hold of life
with grace and determination
making it your own
molding your dreams into reality
I've watched as you fill to the brim
with happiness and pride
with each new accomplishment
I have seen your heart broken
and felt your pain
as the tears spilled from your eyes
I know the sadness that consumes you
when those who are supposed to care
belittle your ambition
trying to take control of your destiny

I've seen traces of doubt begin to invade
tearing at your self-confidence
and I begin to worry that maybe this time
you won't heal
But after allowing yourself
to feel the pain
to cry the tears
you do heal
Stronger and more determined
you tighten your grip on life
leaving the negative behind
My daughter
keep reaching for the stars
and ultimately they will be yours

— Sharon M. McCabe

# Don't Place Limits on Yourself

Let there be many windows
   to your soul,
That all the glory of the universe
May beautify it.

— Ella Wheeler Wilcox

When you place limits on
what you can accomplish,
you wind up cheating yourself
out of amazing opportunities.
Don't let that happen. Don't
allow fear to control what
could be your destiny.

Have faith in yourself and
the discipline to see things
through, and you will see your
life unfold before you. Strive
to do the best you can, and
eventually your dreams will
come true.

— T. L. Nash

# Believe in Yourself, Daughter...

Believe in who you are,
as a free spirit...
Never measure your life
by others' standards,
live according
to your inner spirit,
and dance to your own music.

Live honestly
and accept these gifts...
your beauty,
your differences,
your humanity...
Never doubt yourself,
your call to love,
or choices made.

It is your right on this earth
to stand strong
for what you believe
is your true destiny
and direction.

Do not falter ...or lose heart!

— Pam Reinke

# ...as I Believe
# in You

In your eyes I see...
    Strength and tenderness
    Hope untouched by despair
    Potential

In your mind I see...
    Hunger for truth and knowledge
    Recognition of right and wrong
    Determination

In your heart I see...
    Joy and compassion
    A sense for what is kind and good
    Fearless love

In the stars I see...
    A journey of a thousand
        peaks and valleys
    In a life that is destined
        to be extraordinary

— Pat Fream

# You Really Are
# One of a Kind

You were put on this Earth
with unique talents and abilities.
Your experiences
and your way of seeing the world
are yours — and yours alone.

Honor the precious gifts
    you've been given
by honing and polishing your talents
    until they shine like diamonds.

Celebrate your life —
all that you are
and all you can be —
by granting your soul
the freedom to sing, dance, create,
    soar, and reach for the sky.

Share the beauty you create
and let it light the world
    like a thousand candles.

— Jason Blume

# My Promises to You

When you are happy,
  I'll love you with
    a joyful heart.
When you are sad,
  I'll love you with a heart
  made a little heavier
    by your tears.
When you are right,
  I'll love you with a heart
    filled with pride.
When you are wrong,
  I'll love you with a heart
      that has learned acceptance.

When you succeed,
  I'll love you with a cheering heart.
When you fail,
  I'll love you with a heart that
    rewards the efforts you've made.
When you dream,
  I'll love you with
    an encouraging heart.
When you give up,
  I'll love you with a heart
    that is strong enough
      for both of us.
When you are simply you,
  in whatever mood or phase
    of your life,
  I'll love you with all my heart
    and more than you'll ever know.

— Linda Sackett-Morrison

# You Will Always Be My Beautiful Daughter

I looked at you today
and saw the same beautiful eyes
that looked at me with love
when you were a baby
I looked at you today
and saw the same beautiful mouth
that made me cry when you
    first smiled at me
when you were a baby
It was not long ago
that I held you in my arms
long after you fell asleep
and I just kept rocking you
all night long

I looked at you today
and saw my beautiful daughter
no longer a baby
but a beautiful person
with a full range of emotions
feelings, ideas and goals
Every day is exciting
as I continue to watch you grow
I want you to always know that
in good and in bad times
I will love you
and that no matter what you do
or how you think
or what you say
you can depend on
my support, guidance
friendship and love
every minute of every day
I love being your parent

— Susan Polis Schutz

# No One Will Ever
# Be in My Heart
# the Way You Are

For all the times
Our days were relentless
And things seemed so rushed;

>   For all the times
>   You grew up a little quicker
>   Because I couldn't always be there;

For all the times
You heard me angry and frustrated
Or saw me impatient;

>   For all the times
>   I thought I was listening
>   And realized later I hadn't heard you.

I have cried inside again and again
Because maybe what you didn't see were...

All the times
I laughed and boasted about you,
Your ingenuity, your brilliance;

All the times
I sat with a lump in my throat,
Choking back tears of pride
As I watched you perform;

All the times
I noticed how fast you were growing
And changing into a magnificent,
Separate person;

All the times
I marveled at how perfect you were
As I watched you sleep.

For all the times past
And all the times to come,
No one will ever be in my heart
The way you are.

— Laurie Winkelmann

# Daughter, There Are So Many Things I Wish You Knew...

I wish you knew...

The heartache I feel...
when I watch you struggle with
your disappointments, failures,
or a broken heart.

The sadness I feel...
when I can't rescue you
from your mistakes or pain.

The pride I feel...
when I see your fierce determination
to reach for your goals and dreams.

The joy I feel...
when I see your kindness to others.

The love I feel...
watching you grow
into everything I ever wanted
in a daughter.

I wish you knew...
and now you do.

— Amy D'Agostino

# "Hello, Little One"

Today I looked at your picture
   and whispered, "Hello, little one."
Except you aren't little anymore;
you're all grown up and living your
   own life.
Even though that's exactly what I
   want for you,
there's a part of me that just can't let go
of the child you were.

I remember rocking you to sleep at night
and finding it difficult to put you in
   your crib
because I loved the way you nestled
   against me.
I can still see you learning to crawl.
I remember how you followed me
from room to room,
mimicking everything I did.

I know that life has moved on,
and you are now a woman I can be
proud of,
a woman whose friendship I cherish.
But sometimes
I think back to the days of
your childhood
and I wish I had the chance to do it
all over again.

I want the rest of your life to be filled
with as much love as your heart can hold.
I want you to achieve every goal
you set for yourself.
I want you to know that I will always
love you.
You are the woman I had hoped you
would be —
it just happened faster than I
had anticipated.
So please bear with me if you hear
me whisper, "Hello, little one."

— Lea Walsh

# To a Daughter Leaving Home

When I taught you
at eight to ride
a bicycle, loping along
beside you
as you wobbled away
on two round wheels,
my own mouth rounding
in surprise when you pulled
ahead down the curved
path of the park,
I kept waiting
for the thud
of your crash as I
sprinted to catch up,
while you grew
smaller, more breakable
with distance,
pumping, pumping
for your life, screaming
with laughter,
the hair flapping
behind you like a
handkerchief waving
goodbye.

— Linda Pastan

# Carry These Gifts with You Always

Love — to shine like blue skies above you wherever you go, so that you always know you're in the hearts of so many people.

Light — to see the end of the tunnel when you're struggling with troubles, so you always know you have the inner power to survive and triumph.

Lullabies — to fill your mind with highlights of your childhood, so you focus on the good times and great people who nurtured your growth, smiled on your potential, and walked beside you on all the paths toward your dreams.

Laughter — to keep you healthy in mind and body; to give you the ability to tell great jokes, act silly, and exercise your giggle; to remind you that life is too short to be taken so seriously.

A ladder — tall enough for you to climb so you can reach for your stars.

A lifeline — to anchor you, support you, and keep you going forward in a positive way when you're faced with a crisis, so you always know you are a survivor.

Lots of good luck — to help you fulfill all your wishes, so you always know your possibilities are unlimited — and success is your destiny.

— Jacqueline Schiff

# If Only Time Didn't Have to Go By So Fast

Of course I always knew
that someday you would be
a woman building your own life,
chasing dreams you've spent
    years creating.
You would sit across from me
and smile that smile
that would remind me of when
you were a little girl.
A million memories
would pass through my mind,
and I would be so proud
of who you've become
and so very thankful
to have been blessed with you.
And here we are.
It came just a little too fast —
I always knew it would.
But you are so beautiful,
and every time I look at you,
I am flooded with memories
    of your childhood
and awed by the woman
that you've become.

— Kellie L. McCracken

# *You Have Brought Me So Much Joy*

The greatest gift that a parent can receive is a daughter — a little bundle of pink who wraps her precious life around a parent's heart and brings the most incredible feeling of love into her world.

From that love grows a spunky and happy ponytailed face that fills the home with laughter. The drawings that are still tucked away are just a few of the wonderful memories that a daughter leaves behind.

As she grows and blossoms, a woman begins to shine through — with hopes, dreams, and a determination to make them come alive. She explores her independence but still finds a way to keep her parents close to her heart. She is brilliant and exciting and allows her parents to walk through life beaming with pride.

As a daughter continues to grow, a parent begins to realize that she has succeeded in turning a little girl into a wonderful woman: someone who is beautiful and intelligent and the best friend that anyone could wish for.

— Debra Heintz

# I Hope You Know How Much You Are Loved

You may not understand
just how much your life means
to those around you —
how our days are brighter
    because you're here
and the sound of your laughter
touches the hearts of everyone
    around you.

Your presence adds something special
    and invaluable to the world.
You bring joy to those who love you
and a smile to everyone you meet.
Though you may never realize it,
    your life is a gift that is treasured.

With each new day, I hope
you will know how much
you are loved.

— Star Nakamoto

# These Are My Dreams for You, Daughter

I dream for your happiness. I want you to be happy with who you are and all that your life involves. I dream for you to always know love, for it is what keeps us in touch with all that is real and true. I dream for you to live in peace. I want your life to be balanced.

I dream for you to succeed. I want you to achieve your goals and ambitions and to place your priorities carefully. I dream for you to always have good health and harmonious physical, emotional, and spiritual well-being. I dream for you to have supportive and caring people around you who love you beyond measure. I dream for you to have a solid and secure future. I want good things to come your way and for you to never be in need. I dream for you to have laughter in your life; it is life's natural source for healing.

I dream for you to remain true to yourself. Never lose sight of the wonderful child you once were and the wonderful woman you are today. Remain faithful to your identity, and never let external distractions sway you. Listen to what your heart tells you.

I dream for you to have strength. Life will be good, but there will be tests. I wish for you to build character with life's lessons. Keep your chin up and remain proud.

I dream for you to stay close to me no matter how far away you may be. You're my daughter, and I love you. Nothing and no one will ever change the way I feel about you. You live in my heart. I will always have dreams for you.

— Debbie Burton-Peddle

# Your Happiness Is What I Wish for Most

I wish for you to always see the goodness
    in this world,
to do your part in helping those
    less fortunate,
to walk hand in hand with those
    of less talent,
to follow those with more knowledge,
to be an equal with those who are different.

I wish for you to find your special purpose
        in this world so full of choices
and to help lead those who stray.
I wish for you to become your own individual —
to set yourself apart from those who are
        the same.
I wish for you the self-confidence to say no
        when it is necessary
and the strength to stand alone.
I wish for you the approval of yourself
to love and respect everything that
        you are and will become.
I wish for you to reap the fruits
        of your talents,
to walk with pride down the road of life,
to be humble in your successes,
and to share in the praises and joy of others.

Most of all, I wish for you to be happy.
For when you are happy,
        you have the key that will open all
            of the world's doors to you.
Whatever you decide, whoever you become,
my love for you is unconditional;
my arms and heart are always open to you.
My wishes for you are that you will someday
know the joys that only a daughter can bring
and that all your wishes come true.

                                    — Jackie Olson

# I Am Honored
# and Proud to Be
# a Part of Your Life

You've worked hard and sacrificed a lot to make your dreams come true. You've battled back from setbacks to claim proud moments. You've had challenges and come through them smarter, stronger, and more confident than ever in your ability to master life.

You've had relationships that didn't work out, but you never let your spirits sink; you had the strength to turn those times of tears into learning and growing experiences. You moved on to new heights.

You've never let yourself be defined by a single achievement; you've been a positive presence and have always done your best. You've helped so many and shined your light wherever you went.

You are a credit to our family and the pride that glows in my heart. As you go forward to make more and more of your dreams come true, I hope you feel my hugs supporting you with the warmest love and the closeness of a parent who is so tremendously proud of you.

— Jacqueline Schiff

# Daughter,
# in This Crazy World
# We Live in,
# It's Nice to Know That
# Some Things Will
# Never Change

No matter what is happening in
the world.
No matter what worries or
frustrations creep in.
No matter what glad or sad tidings
come your way.
No matter how many bills come in
the mail.
No matter how good or bad the news
of the day.
No matter whether the weather is
beautiful or not.
No matter how many times your smile
gets lost.
No matter how difficult or demanding
things can be.
No matter what is happening
anywhere at any time...

You will always be in my heart. You
will always be in my thoughts. And
I'll always be wishing I could find
a way to remind you... that you are
the most beautiful and wonderful
daughter there could ever be.

— Douglas Pagels

# *You Are in My Heart Forever*

The first time I held you in my arms and you wrapped your tiny hand around my index finger, I felt my heart swell with immeasurable joy and pride. I knew that my life had been touched in a miraculous way that would transform every dimension of it forever.

From the moment you were born, you became the focal point of my existence. Your smile was the sunshine in my heart. Your happiness was the only treasure I sought.

And so began the great paradox of parenthood. For when your tiny hand touched mine, I knew that I had been chosen to nurture you, love you, and then give you the strength to let go.

Letting go is not easy. But I look at you now — a beautiful young woman, strong in your convictions and determined to face life on your own terms — and I still feel my heart swell with pride and joy.

My dreams for your life might not always be the same ones you seek. But one thing remains the same: your happiness will always be my greatest treasure. I know now that the true miracle of that first touch lies in one simple truth: even though your hand may slip away from mine, we will hold each other in our hearts forever.

— Nancy Gilliam

# Daughter, You Are Life's Greatest Gift to Me

Memories come flooding back to me
    as I look back over the years.
I want to hold on to you
    and at the same time
        watch you fly high and free...

You have such spirit
      and a character all your own.
You are a doer and an achiever
      of what you believe in.
I'm so proud of the dreams you have
      and the conviction you have
to make those dreams come true.
Your world is bright, new,
      and bursting with possibilities.

It's so easy to remember
      your very first steps
and how I held out my hand
      for you to hold.
As each year passes,
       you take more steps,
and some of these will eventually
      lead you away from me —
but always remember that my hand
      and my heart
are forever here for you.
You have been life's greatest gift to me,
      and I love you so much.

— Vickie M. Worsham

# ACKNOWLEDGMENTS

We gratefully acknowledge the permission granted by the following authors, publishers, and authors' representatives to reprint poems or excerpts from their publications.

Loyola Press, www.loyolapress.org, for "One dreams of having a daughter..." from "Dream Weaver" and "Virginia Woolf once said..." from "Homage" from DANCING WITH MY DAUGHTER by Jayne Jaudon Ferrer, Copyright © 2004 by Jayne Jaudon Ferrer. Reprinted by permission. All rights reserved.

Debra Heintz for "Every Day I Am Thankful to Have You as My Child" and "You Have Brought Me So Much Joy." Copyright © 2008 by Debra Heintz. All rights reserved.

Jacqueline Schiff for "I Hope You'll Keep Flying to the Heights of Your Dreams" and "I Am Honored and Proud to Be a Part of Your Life." Copyright © 2008 by Jacqueline Schiff. All rights reserved.

Jenny Scott for "This Girl of Mine." Copyright © 2008 by Jenny Scott. All rights reserved.

BOA Editions, Ltd., www.boaeditions.org, for "For My Daughter Who Loves Animals" from WHAT WE CARRY by Dorianne Laux. Copyright © 1994 by Dorianne Laux. All rights reserved.

Natasha Josefowitz for "My Favorite Woman" from NATASHA'S WORDS FOR FAMILIES. Copyright © 1986 by Natasha Josefowitz. All rights reserved.

Cheryl D'Aprix for "What a Dad Will Do for His Daughter." Copyright © 1998 by Cheryl D'Aprix. All rights reserved.

PrimaDonna Entertainment Corp. for "Life Lessons on the Road to Your Dreams" by Donna Fargo. Copyright © 2008 by PrimaDonna Entertainment Corp. All rights reserved.

T. L. Nash for "When you place limits on...." Copyright © 2008 by T. L. Nash. All rights reserved.

Pam Reinke for "Believe in who you are...." Copyright © 2008 by Pam Reinke. All rights reserved.

Pat Fream for "In your eyes I see...." Copyright © 2008 by Pat Fream. All rights reserved.

Jason Blume for "You Really Are One of a Kind." Copyright © 2008 by Jason Blume. All rights reserved.

Amy D'Agostino for "Daughter, There Are So Many Things I Wish You Knew...." Copyright © 2008 by Amy D'Agostino. All rights reserved.

W. W. Norton & Company, Inc., for "To a Daughter Leaving Home" from THE IMPERFECT PARADISE: POEMS by Linda Pastan. Copyright © 1989 by Linda Pastan. All rights reserved.

Debbie Burton-Peddle for "These Are My Dreams for You, Daughter." Copyright © 2008 by Debbie Burton-Peddle. All rights reserved.

A careful effort has been made to trace the ownership of selections used in this anthology in order to obtain permission to reprint copyrighted material and give proper credit to the copyright owners. If any error or omission has occurred, it is completely inadvertent, and we would like to make corrections in future editions provided that written notification is made to the publisher:

BLUE MOUNTAIN ARTS, INC., P.O. Box 4549, Boulder, Colorado 80306.